15-Minu...

A Way out of Despair

Helena Wilkinson

Copyright © CWR 1995, 2002
First published 1995 as *New Perspectives, A Way Out of Despair*, by CWR. This edition published 2002 by CWR, Waverley Abbey House, Waverley Lane, Farnham, Surrey GU9 8EP. Reprinted 2002, 2003, 2005.

Cover design, internal design and typesetting by Elaine Bond at CWR.

All rights reserved. No part of this publication may be reproduced, stored in a retrieval system, or transmitted, in any form or by any means, electronic, mechanical, photo-copying, recording or otherwise, without the prior permission in writing of CWR.

Unless otherwise identified, all Scripture quotations in this publication are from the *Holy Bible: New International Version* (NIV). Copyright © 1973, 1978, 1984, International Bible Society.

Printed in England by Halstan.
ISBN 1-85345-208-4

Biography

After working as a research assistant in the psychiatric department of a Zulu hospital, Helena trained in counselling. For four years she edited **Carer and Counsellor** and worked for CWR in the editorial and counselling departments. She is the author of six books, including **Puppet on a String**, her account of anorexia, and **Beyond Chaotic Eating**, a Christian approach to eating disorders. Helena is the founder of the Kainos Trust, a Christian charity that supports people with eating disorders through counselling, residential courses, teaching and drop-in days and correspondence. She speaks regularly on eating disorders and related subjects and was recently described as "probably the best eating-disorders counsellor in Europe". Convinced of Jesus' power to heal, Helena speaks with direction and sensitivity.

Day 1
Help!

Well done! It takes courage to pick up a book such as this when in the midst of despair. I want you to know that having taken this step you are not alone.

You may have reached a point, or had odd moments, of not wanting to live any more. Sometimes this is not so much actually wanting to die, as not wanting to live the way you feel at present. It may seem as though things will never change, but believe me, as someone who has walked a similar path in the past, and who has walked with many others, it can be different.

You are not alone

As you walk the path towards healing, walking with you is God. Before we go any further let me remind you of a few things about God. He is:

- unfailing love (Psalm 36:7);
- gracious to you (Isaiah 30:18);
- good to all and has compassion (Psalm 145:9);
- slow to anger (Numbers 14:18);
- rich in mercy (Ephesians 2:4);
- forgiving (1 John 1:9);
- rich in wisdom (Romans 11:33);
- full of grace and truth (John 1:14);
- faithful (Psalm 89:1);
- kind (Psalm 86:5);
- just (Deuteronomy 32:4).

Aren't these the kind of qualities you would want in someone who comes alongside you in a time of despair?

I encourage you to walk one day at a time through the rest of this book knowing that God, who is impartial and loving, will be walking with you every step of the way. As the writer I travel with you too. How? Preparing

> "... save me because of your unfailing love."
> Psalm 6:4

this book has meant spending time getting close to some of what you may now be facing. In the writing I have felt, thought, reflected and prayed. I feel as if a part of me knows you, and I know something of the depth of anguish you are facing.

"I will come to you"

How can God walk with you? The Trinity reveals God the Father, Son and Holy Spirit. The Spirit has been given to us to live in us and guide us. Jesus says, *"And I will ask the Father, and he will give you another Counsellor to be with you for ever – the Spirit of truth. The world cannot accept him, because it neither sees him nor knows him. But you know him, for he lives with you and will be in you. I will not leave you as orphans; I will come to you"* (John 14:16–18).

As you read these words each day, bear in mind that at any point you can ask for the help of the Holy Spirit. He will not invade. You need to ask. We are body, soul and spirit and we have the choice to respond to God through our souls (mind, will, emotions) or through our spirit. We need to communicate with God through our spirits. When our spirits listen to the Holy Spirit, God works powerfully in us because the Holy Spirit guides us in the truth.

For reflection and action

- *Things can be different.*
- *You are not alone in the journey.*
- *The Holy Spirit has been given to you to guide you*
- *At any point you can ask for the help of the Holy Spirit.*

Day 2

Sinking

It may seem that you are at the bottom of a slimy pit. But God is going to set your feet on a rock, a secure place, and put a new song in your mouth. How? Through learning to stand on the truth.

Jesus taught that those who hear His words and put them into practice build their house on the rock. There is a difference between hearing and doing. If we only hear the words but do not put them into practice, it is like having God with us but building on sand. We hold onto Him desperately as we sink!

What is truth? Truth is what God says in His Word. He says a lot about Himself, about His offer to us of being reconciled to Him, and about all that is made available to us through Jesus.

Life in Christ

We read yesterday a few truths about God. Let us now look at what has been accomplished through Jesus' death:

- I have been rescued from the dominion of darkness and brought into the kingdom of the Son (Colossians 1:13);
- I have been redeemed through the blood of Christ and have received forgiveness of my sins (Colossians 1:14);
- I have been reconciled to God through Jesus Christ, without blemish and free from accusation (Colossians 1:22);
- I have been born again of imperishable seed, through the living and enduring Word of God (1 Peter 1:23);
- I have eternal life in Jesus (1 John 5:11).

> **"He lifted me out of the slimy pit, out of the mud and mire; he set my feet on a rock and gave me a firm place to stand. He put a new song in my mouth, a hymn of praise to our God." (Psalm 40:2–3)**

For those who believe this and declare Jesus as Lord much is available to them:

- I have been buried with Christ in baptism and I have been made alive with Christ (Colossians 2:12–13);
- God has poured His love into my heart by the Holy Spirit (Romans 5:5);
- I have been blessed by God with every spiritual blessing (Ephesians 1);
- I am a joint heir with Christ (Romans 8:17).

To know God's empowering we must have been born again and filled with the Holy Spirit. To be born again is to repent of our independence from God and to declare the Lordship of Jesus over our lives. To be filled with the Holy Spirit is to receive through Jesus baptism in the Holy Spirit.

One of the things which often stops us from letting God do His work is wondering how He will do it! The disciples who were told to go out and preach the Word to all the nations might have wondered how they were going to do that too. It so happened that Pentecost occurred on a day when there were people from many different nations right outside their doors! You may wonder how God is going to work it out in your life. Don't try to work out what only God can work out.

For reflection and action

- Ensure that you are born again and filled with the Holy Spirit.
- Make the decision to read the Bible and receive the truth.
- Don't try to work out how God will bring healing and freedom.
- Invite the Holy Spirit to work in your life.

Blackness

A state of blackness can be frightening, like a thick blanket thrown over you, where suddenly all is dark. It is easy to think of black as black. When you look at different colours you can easily see that there are shades of the same colour. It can seem that black, being a neutral colour, doesn't vary. But there are degrees of blackness in colour, and there are degrees of blackness in experience.

Separating the layers of darkness

I worked in a nursery school for a while. Given paper and paint some of the children used to put one colour on top of another until what they were left with was a dark mess. Perhaps that is how your life seems at present: one big mess. If you think of the primary school painting, many layers went into creating the black blob. So often, many layers go into building an emotional state of blackness. It can be helpful to begin to separate out the layers so that each one can be dealt with. There may be a physical, emotional or spiritual component to the problem.

Nothing is impossible to God

One of the difficult aspects of the blackness is the often accompanying lack of energy and lack of interest in things. This is a time when you need someone to stand with you, emotionally and spiritually, and sometimes physically. You may need someone to remind you that what seems impossible to some is never impossible to God. Seek out an anointed person of faith to minister the truth to you, and allow the Holy Spirit to unravel the mess. But remember we cannot do it in our own strength, whether we are the one in need of support or the one supporting someone else. Even Jesus said, "*I tell you the truth, the Son can do nothing by himself; he can only do*

> "Even in darkness light dawns ..."
> Psalm 112:4

what he sees his Father doing, because whatever the Father does the Son also does" (John 5:19). Through God's power released by our faith we can believe that no situation is too difficult for God to overcome. Jesus is the creative Word of God, therefore, He can and will create. He creates, He repairs, He restores. He is in the business of restoring lives and that includes your life!

For reflection and action

- Seek the support of a person with faith who will minister the truth to you.
- Remember, nothing is too difficult for God.
- God is in the business of restoring lives, including yours.
- Have faith to believe that God is setting you free.

Day 4

Grief

Has anyone ever wept with you in your pain? I remember an instance in my life where I was facing deep pain and spoke to a friend. She wept. It was one of the most moving experiences. Do you know that Jesus weeps with you? When Lazarus had died, even though Jesus knew he would be raised from death, He wept. Why? Because He knew the pain of those close to Lazarus. When Jesus saw Mary weeping, and the Jews who had come along with her also weeping, *"he was deeply moved in spirit and troubled ... Jesus wept ... Then the Jews said, 'See how he loved him!'"* (John 11:33–36). Jesus weeps with you because He loves you.

Life-draining

You may feel that while in the middle of grief, you will stay in that state forever. Grief is draining. It takes life from us. Psalm 119:50 says, *"My comfort in my suffering is this: Your promise preserves my life."* What is God's promise? Jesus said, "I have come that they may have life, and have it to the full" (John 10:10).

Do you understand who God really is? He is the One who created the whole of the heavens and the earth. He is powerful! Isaiah 42:5–6 says, *"This is what God the Lord says – he who created the heavens and stretched them out, who spread out the earth and all that comes out of it, who gives breath to its people, and life to those who walk on it: 'I, the Lord, have called you in righteousness; I will take hold of your hand. I will keep you and make you to be a covenant for the people and a light for the Gentiles.'"*

> "Out of the depths I cry to you, O Lord."
> Psalm 130:1

Christ is the answer

Note, God gives breath to His people, and life. He is not going to withhold this from you, you are one of His people. He has called you in righteousness. If you take hold of that righteousness, by walking with Christ, by allowing Him to be your strength, by looking to Him as the answer, God will not only keep you, but you will be a light to people. We tend to think that God only uses a few people to do His work. No! He has a calling upon the life of every believer. Jesus did not say only to some believers that they would do even greater things than He did, through the Holy Spirit, but to all believers. Catch hold of the purposes of God in your life.

There is a difference between crying out to God in our grief, and clinging onto ourselves in our grief. Why is it so important to cry out to God amid our distress, rather than handle it alone? In the first situation we believe for what God is going to do; in the second situation we move into self-pity. Draw on God. Psalm 126:5 reminds us, *"Those who sow in tears will reap with songs of joy"*.

For reflection and action

- Jesus weeps with you because He loves you.
- God's promise renews your life.
- God gives breath and life to His people.
- If you cry out to God, though you sow in tears you will reap in joy.

Day 5
Hopelessness

God has seen your affliction; and He has heard your cry. Exodus 3:7 says, *"The Lord said, 'I have indeed seen the misery of my people in Egypt. I have heard them crying out because of their slave drivers, and I am concerned about their suffering.'"* God has heard you crying out. You may be thinking, "So if God is concerned about my suffering, why doesn't He do something?" Read on, "*'So I have come down to rescue them from the hand of the Egyptians and to bring them up out of that land into a good and spacious land, a land flowing with milk and honey ...'"* (Exodus 3:8).

More than you could ever imagine

God has not just heard your cry, He is going to take you out of your Egypt, out of captivity, and to a good and spacious land. When God gets involved in your rescue, He does not just open the prison door and say, "OK, go!" He says, "Look what I have for you ... more than you could ever imagine". But, it is what He has for us; not what we think is good for us.

If someone asked me what I want right now, I would say, "Marriage and children". I don't have it, and if I focused on not having it then I could become depressed. What is God doing in my life right now? He is stripping down my ministry and building His ministry. I could look at the situation and say, "God has not released me from my captivity, from my state of singleness." In other words it could seem hopeless, but in fact what is happening is one of the most exciting things that has ever happened to me. I am having to learn to trust God in the bigger plan in my life. Although it may feel as if we are consumed by our circumstances, Scripture says that *"Because of the Lord's great love we are not consumed, for his compassions never fail"* (Lamentations 3:22).

> "... he turned to me and heard my cry."
> Psalm 40:1

Therefore I have hope

The writer of Lamentations says of the Lord's compassions, *"They are new every morning; great is your faithfulness"* (Lamentations 3:23). Lamentations is the most melancholy book in the prophets; the writer was totally overwhelmed by the circumstances. You only have to read the words which precede the verses above, *"I remember my affliction and my wandering, the bitterness and the gall. I well remember them, and my soul is downcast within me"* (Lamentations 3:19–20). But, in the midst of his gloom the writer draws on deep hope and trust. He says, *"Yet this I call to mind and therefore I have hope [the Lord's great compassions]"* (Lamentations 3:21).

Remember what the writer of Lamentations said, *"Yet this I call to mind ..."* He had to choose to remember the Lord's compassion, love, mercy; likewise we have to choose to call to mind these things. If we do not remind ourselves then we will be consumed by our circumstances.

For reflection and action

- *God has heard your cry.*
- *God wants to release you from captivity.*
- *Can you learn to trust God in the bigger plan in your life?*
- *Remind yourself of God's compassions each day.*

Day 6

Storm

I was recently driving with a friend when we hit a patch of very dark and heavy clouds. Their formation was such that it felt as if they could quite literally engulf us and suck us into their midst, never to return. Their presence felt oppressive, and as the rain lashed down it seemed determined to obscure our vision. Then I changed my view only slightly and caught sight of the beginnings of a rainbow. As I looked again I saw that it was a double rainbow. I didn't want it to go away and I kept gazing. Still stuck in the storm, but now focusing on the bands of colour, the clouds no longer felt oppressive. I traced the arch of the rainbow up into the blackness and down again. The end of it was piercing a field of green and golden grass with a brilliance I have rarely seen.

The rainbow in the storm

Gradually I saw the whole picture: the beginning and the end of the rainbow and the full arch between the two. Ahead of us was a soft blue sky. That's where we were heading! Although we were still in the clouds, it felt calm. Soon we would leave the blackness behind. Even in the middle of the storm I began to become less and less conscious of it, for I was unable to stop looking at the wonderful sight ahead.

Feeling that the blackness or heaviness will engulf you can be frightening. Psalm 107:28–30 says: "*Then they cried out to the Lord in their trouble, and he brought them out of their distress. He stilled the storm to a whisper; the waves of the sea were hushed. They were glad when it grew calm, and he guided them to their desired haven. Let them give thanks to the Lord for his unfailing love and his wonderful deeds for men.*"

> **"Then the Lord answered Job out of the storm."**
> **Job 38:1**

Focusing on the light of Christ

Fear only remains during the times in which we focus on the darkness. The first step in the psalm was that the people cried out to the Lord. But crying out to the Lord in the darkness needs to be sustained by focusing on the light of Christ. It is so easy to cry out and yet remain in the dark, and in so doing still feel engulfed. As you stare into the blackness it appears to get blacker. As you stare at the storm it can leave you concerned as to what form it will take. As we focus on Jesus, we begin to see His light, and in His light we begin to see the light, we begin to see hope: *"For with you is the fountain of life; in your light we see light"* (Psalm 36:9).

Following the crying out to the Lord and His calming the storm, the psalm says that the people were glad that it grew calm, and God guided them to their desired haven. As we cry out and begin to see change, however small, we need to respond with gladness and thanks for God's unfailing love.

For reflection and action

- *Cry out to God.*
- *Change your view, if only slightly.*
- *Keep focusing on the light of Christ.*
- *Remember, where there is light it is never fully dark. Give thanks.*

Day 7
Desperation

Do you feel so desperate that at times you feel inconsolable? Perhaps it's difficult to know what to do. There is a course of action you can follow.

Nehemiah had a situation to deal with – he had to rebuild the walls of Jerusalem – and he had opposition. Do you have a problem and do you have opposition? Perhaps the combination of the problem and the opposition causes you to feel like giving up. What did Nehemiah do? He took his problem to the Lord and the Lord answered him. It is worth reading Nehemiah's prayer in chapter 1. He didn't just say, "O God, sort it out." Look at how he began, *"O Lord, God of heaven, the great and awesome God, who keeps his covenant of love with those who love him and obey his commands, let your ear be attentive and your eyes open to hear the prayer your servant is praying before you day and night …"* (Nehemiah 1:5–6). He worshipped, he cried out, he prayed over and over. Before he goes on to ask the Lord again to answer, he confesses the sins that the Israelites, including himself and his father's house, have committed against God. This is also important.

Persistent prayer

Nehemiah's prayer was a persistent prayer from the heart which reverenced God. Consequently he saw a result. When he knew God was giving him success, despite opposition, he got on with the job. He took action! We need to make sure that when we pray we expect something to happen and we take action. We mustn't just sit and wait, but believe that God has heard and begin to respond accordingly

> "My soul is in anguish ... I am worn out from groaning; all night long I flood my bed with weeping and drench my couch with tears."
> (Psalm 6:3, 6)

The joy of the Lord is our strength

Nehemiah understood God's provision and understood from where his strength came. In chapter 8 verse 10 Nehemiah says, "... *the joy of the Lord is your strength*". Incidentally, Nehemiah means "Jehovah comforts". He does! When in despair we can feel lethargic and drained, but as we focus on God, worship Him, allow the love of God to permeate, and the joy to grow out of that love, we will find that we are sustained through the situation. It is easy to ask God to do something and then to take our eyes off God. But, the key is that our strength is found in the joy of the Lord, not in the resolution of the problem.

For reflection and action

- *Take the problem to the Lord.*
- *Pray persistently, first reverencing God.*
- *Believing God has heard, take action.*
- *Our strength is found in the joy of Lord, not the resolution of the problem.*

Day 8

Condemnation

How often have you felt condemned by others? How often do you condemn yourself? I put the latter in the present tense because for many people condemning oneself is an ongoing process.

Much of our self-condemnation, and condemnation from others, is in connection with doing something wrong or failing to put into practice the truth of God's Word. If we look at Jesus and His way of handling situations where people have been trapped in unhelpful behaviour patterns, we see a person who displayed an incredibly merciful attitude, and yet did not condone wrong-doing.

In John 8 the teachers of the Law and the Pharisees brought before Jesus a woman caught in adultery, for which the penalty was to be stoned to death. *"Jesus bent down and started to write on the ground with his finger. When they kept on questioning him, he straightened up and said to them, 'If any one of you is without sin, let him be the first to throw a stone at her'"* (vv. 6–7). All the people left, until only Jesus and the woman were together. *"Jesus straightened up and asked her, 'Woman, where are they? Has no-one condemned you?' 'No-one, sir,' she said. 'Then neither do I condemn you.' Jesus declared. 'Go now and leave your life of sin'"* (vv.10–11).

Grace and mercy

The woman had been let off the death penalty. At that moment she knew grace and mercy in forgiveness. I am sure that knowing from what she had been spared caused her to turn from her ways.

I guess the difference for us is that without such a cost for our wrong-doing, we can view sin lightly not realising the penalty from which we have been freed.

> **"Therefore, there is now no condemnation for those who are in Christ Jesus." Romans 8:1**

We need to take into ourselves God's grace and mercy. Grace and mercy are words that we may not really understand. God's mercy is evidence of His compassion. Compassion is not feeling sorry for, it is to come and suffer alongside. God becomes involved; He reaches out to meet our needs. Mercy is tender, and through His mercy we see that God is tender-hearted. God is tender-hearted towards you.

God doesn't have to do anything to be merciful; He already is merciful. But we have to do something; we have to receive His mercy. It sounds easy, but many hold back. Why? Because they come to God with their hands clasped tightly – full of anger, sorrow, pain, fear, and don't hold out their hands to receive.

Think of the woman caught in adultery. Would she have said to Jesus, "I can't believe that you haven't condemned me so I shall take the stoning instead of the freedom and path of righteousness?" No! She knew that she had been given another chance – and she received. Will you allow yourself another chance?

For reflection and action

- *Our unhelpful behaviour can be wrong-doing or failing to put into practice the truth of God's Word.*
- *Do you know that God has spared you the death penalty through His Son?*
- *Are you willing to receive God's grace and mercy?*
- *Are you willing to give yourself another chance?*

Day 9

Emptiness

Much of the emptiness which results in deep inner pain has to do with unmet needs. When God made man He made him with different needs: identity; significance; security; self-worth.

We were made to be dependent on God. Sin came in the way and the essence of sin is independence: "I can meet my own needs". So,

identity	became	identity crisis
significance	became	insignificance
security	became	insecurity
self-worth	became	inferiority

Meeting your needs

We are born into the post-Fall era (identity crisis, etc), and we try to meet those needs. And there is nothing wrong in reaching out for needs to be met: the Bible talks about man being hungry and thirsty. The problem comes in where we look – to ourselves or to others. What God says is, "Turn to me."

The legacy of the Fall has to be put to death. Many of us know this is so if we are to live in abundant life. But there is more – and this many of us find harder – our attempts to meet those needs have to die too. This means wrong behaviour, ways of relating, compulsions, dependency on others and independence, etc.

If you think there is no solution you will not let go. But there is a solution! Although we were born into the legacy of the Fall, when we became born again something happened! It is not something that will happen as we develop, it has already happened. Romans 6 teaches us of a new foundation to our lives.

Our old nature has been taken to the cross and it has been killed. You may not feel as if your old nature is dead, but it is dead. We have died with Christ and we have been buried with Him. Someone once said, "The whole point of

> "... you were redeemed from the empty way of life ... ."
> 1 Peter 1:18

a burial is that you say goodbye." So, we say goodbye to our identity crisis, insignificance, etc. It is easy to kill off the old identity and then not bury it ... but there needs to be death and burial of the old identity so that there can be resurrection of the new identity. Our identity in Christ. If you then try to meet your own needs, you are denying that God has dealt with the old.

The bottom of the pit

The bottom of a pit seems the emptiest place on earth. But at the bottom of the pit we cry for help. You have the opportunity now to recognise that you can let go of your own efforts and let God step in. In 2 Corinthians 1: 8–9 Paul says, "... *We were under great pressure, far beyond our ability to endure, so that we despaired even of life. Indeed, in our hearts we felt the sentence of death ...* " (Is that how you feel?) "*But this happened that we might not rely on ourselves but on God, who raises the dead.*"

The opposite of empty is full. What should we be filled with? The Holy Spirit. What you are full of is what you will overflow with!

For reflection and action

- *Are you aware of the ache of needs in your life?*
- *God says, "Turn to me to have your needs met."*
- *At the bottom we cry for help.*
- *Are you prepared to let go of your own efforts?*

Day 10

Doubt

Sometimes, in moments of despair, it can feel as if everything has gone, even God. At other times it seems not so much that everything has gone, but that everything has changed, and suddenly we are left feeling unsure as to how the jigsaw of life fits together.

"Doubt and yet believe"

Spiritual doubt frequently occurs at a time in our lives when we are needing to make changes, spiritually or emotionally. Is this a time when change needs to take place in your life? If so, it is a time to be glad. You have the opportunity to move into a new dimension of faith. I remember when I first became a Christian hearing someone sing the words "thank you for the faith to doubt and yet believe". It mystified me. As the years have gone on I have discovered that in many ways we can believe for the sake of believing, but sometimes when we have doubted we discover a new depth to believing.

There is a difference between doubt and unbelief. Doubt has to do with questioning, whereas unbelief has to do with ruling out. Doubt is when you have had faith and have let go of it. Unbelief is an absence of faith. In a time of darkness you can wonder if God is there. Think of Joseph in prison. God did not speak to him in the way He had done with Abraham, Isaac and Jacob. But God had given him a promise, and as it says in Genesis 39:20–21, "... *while Joseph was there in the prison, the Lord was with him* ..." The same is true for you. Do you know that the presence of God is with you? You may say, "God hasn't given me any promises." The Word of God holds many promises for you.

> "Be merciful to those who doubt ..."
> Jude v.22

Water in a parched land

Doubt can become the wave which casts us ruthlessly on the rocks of life and leaves us to dry out, or it can become the wave which draws us back into the life-giving water where we discover afresh the wonder of moisture in a parched land. *"Jesus stood and said in a loud voice, 'If anyone is thirsty, let him come to me and drink. Whoever believes in me, as the Scripture has said, streams of living water will flow from within him.' By this he meant the Spirit, whom those who believed in him were later to receive ..."* (John 7:37–39). In the desert there is a need to drink. If we do not drink, we remain thirsty.

For reflection and action

- Spiritual doubt often seems to occur at a time of need for change.
- Get to know God's promises for you in Scripture.
- On hearing the Word, don't wait until you feel or understand, but step out believing.
- Allow doubt to be the tool to throw you into a deeper relationship with God

Day 11

Self-Hatred

Self-hatred is one of the bigger battles you are probably facing, especially if you have ever considered suicide. Do you feel useless, a failure, a burden, in battle?

There is tremendous power in the spoken word. The words we speak over ourselves become soaked into our spirits. If a child is told consistently that he is "no good" or "bad", he will believe it and act accordingly. We need to choose to feed into ourselves the truth about ourselves, not a pack of lies! Each time you speak the negative you place yourself under the lie; under a curse. We should never speak that which is a contradiction to God's Word. That's a challenge!

Know who you are in Christ

So, what are some of the truths about you according to God's Word? In Christ you: are a new creation; the old has gone, the new has come (2 Corinthians 5:17); have been given fulness in Christ, who is the head over every power and authority (Colossians 2:10); are reconciled to God and you are righteous in Christ (2 Corinthians 5:20–21); are redeemed from the curse of the law (poverty, sickness, spiritual death) (Galatians 3:13); are God's child (Romans 8:16).

Your wholeness hinges on what you say. James likens the tongue to a bit in a horse's mouth, or the rudder of a ship: it directs the whole course by only a slight movement. So, only a slight negative word about ourselves will result in our feeling negative.

When I repented over all the negative things I had said about myself, including "I wish I were dead", I found myself weeping and weeping. The tears were not of self-hatred, shame or pity, but were tears given by the Holy Spirit – tears of sorrow and healing – as I began to choose to speak the truth about who I am in Christ. We can't wait until we feel like letting go of self-hatred; we will wait forever. I remember someone saying, "God blesses the person who says not 'I want to do your will' but 'I choose to do your will.'"

> "... speaking the truth in love, we will in all things grow up into him ... ."
> **Ephesians 4:15**

Living in Christ

Maybe you back up your philosophy of self-hatred by misunderstanding some of Jesus' words about denying yourself (Matthew 16:24). What Jesus meant was to let go of trying to do it your way! As Neil Anderson says in his book *The Bondage Breaker*,[1] "Jesus was talking about denying yourself in the essential battle of life: the scramble for the throne ...".

We are nothing outside of God, that is why God calls us to put to death the flesh and live in Christ, so that He may see Christ in us. If you put the flesh to death, then there is nothing to hate, because it is gone and now you live in Christ. Our acceptance is by God's grace. The most meaningful explanation I heard of God's grace is, "God giving His everything to those who deserve nothing". None of us deserves, but God gives freely to those who choose to receive.

For reflection and action

- *There is power of blessing and curse in the spoken word.*
- *Confess anything negative as sin, and speak the truth.*
- *Put the flesh and your own efforts to death and live by the Spirit.*
- *Like everyone else, you deserve nothing, but by God's grace He has given you everything. Praise God*

Day 12

Suicide

For some, life reaches a stage where they begin to believe that death is the only way out. Consequently guilt, shame and feelings of failure as a Christian are added. Suicide isn't a word which many feel they can speak in Christian circles. Because of this it remains in the dark and is, therefore, in the devil's camp. It needs to be brought out into the light.

When facing difficult feelings, particularly feelings of suicide, it is easy to assume that this is not something men and women of God have faced, that suicide did not occur in the Bible. Many people think that the only person who committed suicide was Judas Iscariot, and he was the person who betrayed Jesus. You then associate yourself with him: "I'm the scum of the earth."

In the Old Testament a number of cases of suicide were reported: Samson (Judges 16:30); Ahithophel (2 Samuel 17:23); Zimri (1 Kings 16:18); Saul, and Saul's armour bearer (1 Samuel 31:4–5).

No other solution?

To consider suicide does not mean that you are the scum of the earth; it means that you have lost hope, that it feels as if there is no other solution.

There are lots of reasons why a person attempts suicide, apart from really trying to kill him/herself. It can be: a cry for help; a desire for response in others; a need to end pain; a wanting rest and sleep; an addiction to self-harm; an addiction to danger; an act of anger or revenge; a sign of desperation; a state of confusion; a longing to join a loved one.

Maybe you have cried out to God to take your life, attempted to take, or thought about taking your life. Maybe you have harmed yourself in some way.

Did you have a deep experience of God and then later, when faced with suicidal thoughts, wonder what happened? There are several characters in the Bible who were real men of God, who had good beginnings and bad

> "I have had enough, Lord ... Take my life ... ."
> 1 Kings 19:4

times. Why? Because God planted a seed and the people did not let the seed grow. Saul was such a person. He was tall, brave and handsome. He had been anointed with oil by Samuel to be the first king of Israel. But he forsook God's directives and ignored the counsel of Samuel. He sank lower and lower spiritually and his independence got between him and God. In the end he took his life.

Come and lean on God

Are you sinking lower spiritually? Come afresh to God and allow your dependence to be upon Him. Then you will be able to testify, as it says in Psalm 118:17, "*I will not die but live, and will proclaim what the Lord has done*".

For reflection and action

- *Bring your thoughts of suicide out of the darkness into the light.*
- *Repent and ask God's forgiveness for attempting to take your life, or harm yourself in any way.*
- *Receive your forgiveness.*
- *Come afresh to God and depend on Him.*

Day 13

Fight

That you have picked up a book on despair and suicide indicates that you feel there is a battle taking place. You do not have to fight it alone. Indeed, if you attempt to do so you will be overpowered. Ecclesiastes 4:12 says, *"Though one may be overpowered, two can defend themselves. A cord of three strands is not quickly broken."*

The armour of God

Whatever our battle, whether spiritual, emotional or even physical, we need to put on the whole armour of God. Why is it so important? What soldier would enter the battle field unprotected? Yet many people do just that on a daily basis and then wonder why they feel so terrible.

In Ephesians 6 Paul lists six pieces of armour worn by the Roman soldiers at the time: the helmet, breastplate, belt, shoes, shield and the sword. Paul puts these in a spiritual context and tells us to take them to ourselves for defence in spiritual warfare. He warns us "*... our struggle is not against flesh and blood, but against the rulers, against the authorities, against the powers of this dark world and against the spiritual forces of evil in the heavenly realms*" (Ephesians 6:12). We need to take up our defence every day, otherwise we weaken our position. Soldiers put on their armour before they go to war, not during or after.

Into action

Say each day, "*I stand firm with: the belt of truth buckled around my waist; the breastplate of righteousness in place; my feet fitted with the readiness that comes from the gospel of peace; the shield of faith to extinguish all flaming arrows of the evil one; the helmet of salvation; the sword of the Spirit, which is the Word of God.*" To this Paul adds that we should pray in the Spirit on all occasions with all kinds of prayers and requests. We must not just say these things, but do them.

> "... fight the good fight, holding on to faith ... ."
> 1 Timothy 1:18 –19

For the soldier in battle, the helmet protected the brain. One of our most vulnerable parts is the mind, listening to the enemy's lies. The breastplate is the covering of Christ's righteousness, by which alone we are acceptable to God. The belt had to be well-fitting or else the soldier could not walk freely, and we need to keep the truth of God's Word close to us all the time. The shield covered the whole body and it was life or death to the one in battle. Our shield is our faith, but we need to use it for protection. We also need to choose to use the sword, the Word of God, to speak over ourselves the words which God speaks. And as we walk around in our armour we mustn't forget that we walk with our feet fitted with peace.

When Jesus was tempted by Satan, He answered each time with the truth of God's Word. "*Then the devil left him, and angels came and attended him*" (Matthew 4:11). Speaking the truth is our weapon. It is the truth that sets us free.

For reflection and action

- You are in a battle!
- Put on the armour of God every day.
- Pray on all occasions, as though in a battle. Declare victory.
- When tempted by Satan, always speak the truth of God's Word.

Day 14

Trapped

I remember watching on TV the rescue of a man trapped down a sewage pipe. Only the top of his chest, his head and his arms were not submerged. If he hadn't kept his arms in the right position he would have fallen completely. Maybe that's how you feel emotionally – another small movement and you will go under? The man could not pull himself out. His freedom involved the Fire Brigade.

God rescues and saves

Daniel 6:27 says of God "*He rescues and he saves.*" Do you believe that God is going to rescue you from going under? Just as in the rescue of this man other people were brought in, so God sometimes uses His people to be agents for His work. But, it is the work of God, not of the people.

Perhaps you are wondering whether He will save you. If you were a parent and you had two children, both of whom were trapped, you wouldn't rescue one and leave the other! God will not ignore you. When the trapped man was being rescued he had to keep on calling for help. He had to claim his rescue. While people around meant well, they could only comfort him. He needed the Fire Brigade! In the same way you need to call upon God.

We have to understand exactly what is going to rescue us. We know who is going to rescue us: God. We know why: "*'Because he loves me,' says the Lord, 'I will rescue him; I will protect him, for he acknowledges my name'*" (Psalm 91:14). But what brings about the rescue? The price that Jesus paid on the cross: the blood of Jesus. We so often claim the love of Jesus, but it is His blood which has saved us. It is His blood which cleanses us from all unrighteousness. It is His blood which breaks strongholds and sets us free. As a believer you have the right to break every curse over your life: "In the name and through the blood of Jesus I break every curse over my life." It is done! Cover yourself in the blood of Jesus every day.

> "... escape from the trap of the devil, who has taken them captive ... ."
> 2 Timothy 2:26

Take hold of the truth

You need to proclaim what He has done for you through His blood. Not ask timidly that you may be released from the feeling of being trapped. Don't just think things to God, speak them out.

One of the reasons we can feel trapped is due to being in bondage. It says in 2 Peter 2:19 "... *for a man is a slave to whatever has mastered him.*" When we let go of the truth and allow other things to take a hold, that is exactly what they do – take hold! Soon the war we are fighting is not just one of choice, but is a spiritual battle.

Neil Anderson in his book *The Bondage Breaker*[2] talks of various steps to freedom. If being trapped rings true for you, I recommend you read the book.

For reflection and action

- *Call upon God as your helper.*
- *Claim the blood of Jesus over yourself.*
- *Repent of any known sin.*
- *When you have repented, the slate is clean. You start afresh.*

Day 15

Purposelessness

Do you wonder if there is any purpose to your life? Losing someone close, a change in circumstances, trauma, can all evoke feelings of purposelessness; leave you wondering what the point of life is. Not just whether life is worth living, but what the point of it is now, for you.

Hope and a future

Jeremiah 29:11 says, "*'For I know the plans I have for you', declares the Lord, 'plans to prosper you and not to harm you, plans to give you hope and a future.'*" When things change it is easy to feel that we do not fit into the plans of life any more. It is important to hold on to the truth that God has a unique plan for each person's life. There is purpose and direction. Sometimes it takes time to know the plan, or to see the evidence. Abraham was given a purpose by God, that he would father a child. The time gap between God's promise to Abraham and his fathering Isaac was 25 years! That could have been 25 years of discouragement or 25 years of faith-building.

Waiting for a vision to be fulfilled, or to see God's plan for your life as an individual, following a change in life, is not easy, but you need to hold onto the knowledge of the purpose of God in your life.

God's chosen one

Isaiah 42 is the first of several servant songs in that section of Isaiah. It talks of God's promise concerning His servant. Do you know that you are God's servant? Although the passage possibly speaks of Jesus, we who are in Christ are God's servants. Be encouraged by the opening words, "*Here is my servant, whom I uphold, my chosen one in whom I delight; I will put my Spirit*

> "... called according to his purpose."
> **Romans 8:28**

on him and he will bring justice to the nations" (Isaiah 42:1). Look at the words carefully. You are God's servant. God upholds you. You are His chosen one in whom He delights. And He has a purpose for you. Through the Holy Spirit you can accomplish His call on your life.

For reflection and action

- *God's plans are to prosper you and to give you hope.*
- *God upholds you and He will do so in these circumstances.*
- *God chose you and He delights in you.*
- *God has a purpose for you.*

Day 16

Endlessness

Probably one of the most difficult aspects of experiencing desperation is the feeling that you will be stuck in this state day after day. In the midst of winter it is so often difficult to imagine summer.

If we look at the nature of God, who is love, we see that it goes against His nature for us to remain captive to desperation. And yet my trying to reassure you that this time of desperation will end can seem futile.

Let me tell you something which God did in my life, in the hope that it will bring encouragement. I had been going through an exceptionally painful time during which my focus became more on my problems than on God; consequently I began to feel worse. Convinced that this was endless it felt as if life itself was not worth living.

There will be an end

God showed me something I needed to put in order (which I will tell you about another day) and then, in an attempt to be rid of the terrible feelings, I asked someone to pray with me. God worked miraculously as this person ministered the truth of God's Word. A number of days later the Lord gave the same lady a word for me from Nahum "... *He will make a complete end of it. Distress will not rise up twice*" (1:9, NASB). God had shown her that He would complete the work He had begun the day we prayed and that I would never be taken back to the place I had previously been in. She did not know the wording in the version of my Bible and was surprised to find that "distress" appeared where "affliction" appeared in her version. Distress described exactly what I had experienced over the months. Just as apt was the meaning of Nahum: "consolation" or "full of comfort".

> "... he who stands firm to the end will be saved."
> **Matthew 10:22**

Hold on

At the time of going through the distress I was introduced to a woman around my own age who had struggled with emotional problems for a long time. Only a couple of weeks after getting to know her she took her life. Often I walk into town and think of her. I think of how different things are for me now and how they could have been for her too. In a moment of feeling that a situation is endless, don't take an irreversible step as she did.

There will be an end to the current situation, but one day, when there is a new heaven and a new earth, there will be an end to all suffering when God promises that *"He will wipe every tear from their eyes. There will be no more death or mourning or crying or pain, for the old order of things has passed way"* (Revelation 21:4).

For reflection and action

- *Remind yourself of the nature of God – love.*
- *God completes the work He begins in your life.*
- *Don't take an irreversible step.*
- *There will be an end to your current situation.*

Day 17

Powerlessness

Yes, we are powerless in our own right! But God does not say, "My power is made perfect in your strength", but "your weakness".

Only as we are weak do we see God's strength worked out in our lives. Why? Because otherwise it is our strength, not God's. Yet in life so often it is in our times of weakness that others encourage us to become stronger, more self-reliant, more able to solve our problems.

Renew your strength

If we hit rock bottom and admit defeat we can come to God and allow the Holy Spirit to work: "*... but those who hope in the Lord will renew their strength. They will soar on wings like eagles; they will run and not grow weary, they will walk and not be faint*" (Isaiah 40:31). Apparently the eagle is the only bird which renews its strength, renews its wings. As it gets older its wings begin to make a noise and its beak grows callouses, which means that it is less able to catch its prey. So it takes itself off somewhere safe and plucks out all its feathers and rubs the growth off its beak. New feathers grow. We need to go through a similar process: to shed our feathers, let go of what we have relied on to survive, and let God give us His feathers.

Maybe you don't know the authority and power that is rightfully yours through Christ (once born again). Colossians says, "*For in Christ all the fulness of the Deity lives in bodily form, and you have been given fulness in Christ, who is the head over every power and authority*" (2:9–10).

Power within

God is able to do far more than we can ask or imagine according to the power that is at work within us. But, who has to get the power working? We do, by our faith! "I don't feel as if I have the faith to see my problems

> "My grace is sufficient for you, for my power is made perfect in weakness." 2 Corinthians 12:9

through", you may say. But if Jesus is the head over all power and authority and He lives in you, this gives you power and authority. In order to exercise authority, a person has to submit to a higher authority. As you submit to Jesus in each area of your life, so you can command anything which is not of Him to go. The secret is not to say, "I believe it will change", but to command in the name of Jesus for it to change, and then live in the truth that it has changed.

For reflection and action

- *God's power is made perfect in our weakness.*
- *Those who put their hope in the Lord will renew their strength.*
- *You have all power and authority through Christ.*
- *Begin to pray into your situation with that authority!*

Day 18

Alone

Do you feel abandoned by people in the midst of your pain? Or do you feel abandoned on the inside, even though others care?

For some, loneliness can be an infrequent experience which feels uncomfortable, but is not devastating; for others the river of loneliness runs deep, carving great cavities in their lives. Many panic that there is nothing to relieve the terrible ache. Loneliness is not merely a feeling, it's an experience. To be left by oneself is to feel lonely; to ache all over, whether alone or with others, is to know loneliness.

The Lord will never leave you

Do you feel crippled by an inner ache and long for it to change? Where many people turn away from supporting you, or give up on you, God will never turn away. "*The Lord himself goes before you and will be with you; he will never leave you nor forsake you. Do not be afraid; do not be discouraged*" it says in Deuteronomy 31:8.

Jesus experienced the most agonising form of loneliness, which none of us will ever have to face: separation from the Father. He cried, "*My God, my God, why have you forsaken me?*" (Mark 15:34). Someone suggested that it wasn't the crucifixion which killed Jesus, but the weight of the sins; His spirit was broken. Scripture tells us that God is a Father to the fatherless and that He sets the lonely in families (Psalm 68:5). It was never His intention that we should be alone. That's one of the reasons why the church community is so important. He has given us a triangle of relationship: God, neighbour, self.

God has promised us, "*Never will I leave you; never will I forsake you*" (Hebrews 13:5). We need to respond to God's promise, as the passage in Hebrews goes on to say, "So we say with confidence, '*The Lord is my helper; I will not be afraid ...*'" (13:6).

> **"I will not leave you as orphans; I will come to you."**
> **John 14:18**

The effect of loneliness is like a plant deprived of water. The plant quickly droops and loses its strength and its ability to stand. When watered it changes in nature: it stands tall and the leaves become healthy.

The comfort of the Holy Spirit

There is a part of loneliness which is spiritual, deep within our spirits. Our spirits cry out for nourishment, but sometimes we only feed the soul. If you look at the needs of the plant, you could say that light is vital: light can be like nourishment found in relating to others. But without water the plant still dies. It's also not sufficient if the plant just knows it needs water. Unless it receives it, it still dies.

Jesus left us with the Holy Spirit, who is with us at all times. The Holy Spirit is described as the Helper, Counsellor, Teacher, Guide, Discloser. He is also described as the Comforter. Do you know the comfort of the Holy Spirit?

For reflection and action

- *God will never leave you.*
- *Respond to God's promise by turning to Him as your helper.*
- *Receive spiritual nourishment through teaching and worship.*
- *Receive the comfort of the Holy Spirit.*

Worry

Do you worry about how things will work out? Matthew 6 contains Jesus' words of revelation concerning worry. In the NIV the heading is "Do Not Worry". In my Bible, the NASB, the title is, "The Cure for Anxiety". I like that because it offers hope; there is an answer! Don't you sometimes think, "I wish there was an answer?" You probably know Jesus' words well, " ... *do not worry about your life, what you will eat or drink; or about your body, what you will wear. Is not life more important than food, and the body more important than clothes? Look at the birds of the air; they do not sow or reap or store away in barns, and yet your heavenly Father feeds them. Are you not much more valuable than they? Who of you by worrying can add a single hour to his life?*" (Matthew 6:25–27).

Wrong focus

Does that seem hard? It is easy to brush Jesus' words aside, thinking that His teaching is just about not worrying because God will take care of your needs. And yet you question why it hasn't worked out in practical terms. To me the passage speaks of where our focus is. Jesus is reminding us that worry belongs to our focus on the desires of the flesh. But He is calling us to a different place. There can be a relationship with God where we can be caught up and carefree. How? Through allowing Him to bring our spirits to life. We all have spirits, and when we are born again they are awakened. But He wants them to be more than awake, He wants them to be alive. Can you begin to notice the difference between trying to relate to God through your soul (the mind, will and emotions) and communicating with God in your spirit?

> "Cast all your anxiety on him because he cares for you."
> 1 Peter 5:7

Let Jesus take your load

When in the midst of despair it can seem as though you work and work at change and yet very little seems to happen. The "working at it" soon becomes a burden. Jesus says, *"Come to me, all you who are weary and burdened, and I will give you rest. Take my yoke upon you and learn from me, for I am gentle and humble in heart, and you will find rest for your souls. For my yoke is easy and my burden is light"* (Matthew 11:28–30). Jesus' burden is light and in Him there is rest for the weary. Doesn't it feel exhausting carrying your load? Come to Him; let Him take it from you.

Allowing Jesus to take the load involves "letting go". It means no longer trying to do things our way, but allowing the Holy Spirit to have control and to minister in the situation. In Galatians Paul speaks about the flesh and about the Spirit. He describes the manifestations of the flesh as works and the manifestations of the Spirit as fruit. The first requires effort; the second involves surrender. If you are tired of working at your problem, surrender it to God.

For reflection and action

- There is a cure for anxiety!
- God is calling us to be caught up with Him.
- Allowing Jesus to take the load involves "letting go".
- Surrender your problem to God.

Day 20

Fear

Elijah ran away from a situation in fear! A prophet of God, he fled from Jezebel and cried out to God to take his life. "*Elijah was afraid and ran for his life ... into the desert. He came to a broom tree, sat down under it and prayed that he might die. 'I have had enough, Lord,' he said. 'Take my life; I am no better than my ancestors.' Then he lay down under the tree and fell asleep*" (1 Kings 19:3–5). Elijah didn't die. Later an angel spoke to him and the Lord appeared to him.

God is in control

Elijah was a man who was greatly used by the Lord but who attempted to find happiness in success rather than in God. That is why, when a difficult situation came, he fled! We need to find our happiness and our worth as people in God, and as we do so, and really believe that God is in control, fear cannot have a hold on our lives.

Colin Urquhart points out in his book *The Truth That Sets You Free*, "Fear is a soulish reaction either to certain thoughts or words (often inspired by the enemy), or to circumstances. Negative thoughts cause feelings of fear which can easily overwhelm a person. It is common for Christians to seek ministry for their 'fears', even to believe they need to be delivered from a spirit of fear. This is not usually the true nature of the problem ...

"Why does he live in fear then? Because he allows his soul to dominate his spirit, instead of living in submission to God. So the life of his spirit is not able to influence his soul in the way God intends. Within his spirit there is power, love and a sound mind; but these qualities will not be real in his soul unless the Spirit has the pre-eminence in his life."[3]

> **"Be strong, do not fear, your God will come … ."**
> **Isaiah 35:4**

Fear is not from God

We do not live in fear. But one of the tactics of the enemy is to cause us to think that we do. When we feel under attack from fear we have the power to command the fear to leave. We also have to keep reminding ourselves *"… God did not give us a spirit of timidity, but a spirit of power, of love and of self-discipline"* (2 Timothy 1:7). *"For you did not receive a spirit that makes you a slave again to fear, but you received the Spirit of sonship"* (Romans 8:15).

Can you speak those words over yourself? "I do not have a spirit of fear, but I have a spirit of power, of love and of self-discipline." As you say it, begin to take hold of it, your feelings will eventually catch up.

Psalm 91 is a psalm of protection. It says, *"He who dwells in the shelter of the Most High will rest in the shadow of the Almighty. I will say of the Lord, 'He is my refuge and my fortress, my God, in whom I trust'"* (Psalm 91:1–2). When you find somewhere to shelter, you choose to go there because you know that it is safe. Every time you leave the safe place you put yourself at risk of fear.

For reflection and action

- Know that God is in control.
- Be in submission to God and let your spirit be in control of your soul.
- Speak the truth over yourself, despite your feelings.
- Find your shelter in God.

Day 21

Suffering

When suffering overflows it can feel as if it overwhelms. But just as suffering overflows, so does comfort. The image is that it surrounds us, envelopes us, like a river of love which floods over the wounded one, washing away the pain.

God is in control

How we react when things happen to us is important. I remember someone once speaking on Romans 8:28. *"And we know that in all things God works for the good of those who love him, who have been called according to his purpose."* The speaker pointed out that when God says all, He means all. So often we want to know what God's will is; it is that we give thanks in all things. God is the Almighty God and that is why we thank Him. He is in control, and as we thank Him in the circumstance, we acknowledge that.

Do you find it hard to thank God in the situation you are currently in? It is not the sort of prayer which comes naturally, but then neither does forgiveness following hurt. The speaker talked of a couple whose daughter was in a psychiatric hospital in a very bad state. They had prayed and prayed. Then someone said they should give thanks. The day they gave thanks the doctors rang and said, "There is nothing wrong with your daughter."

Streams in the desert

Something happens in the spiritual realm when we give praise in tribulation. When we read parts of Isaiah 35 we see a glimpse of what happens: *"The desert and the parched land will be glad; the wilderness will rejoice and blossom. Like the crocus, it will burst into bloom; it will rejoice*

> "For just as the sufferings of Christ flow over into our lives, so also through Christ our comfort overflows" (2 Corinthians 1:5).

greatly and shout for joy. The glory of Lebanon will be given to it, the splendour of Carmel and Sharon; they will see the glory of the Lord, the splendour of our God.

"Strengthen the feeble hands, steady the knees that give way; say to those with fearful hearts, 'Be strong, do not fear; your God will come ...'

"Then will the eyes of the blind be opened and the ears of the deaf unstopped. Then will the lame leap like a deer, and the mute tongue shout for joy. Water will gush forth in the wilderness and streams in the desert" (Isaiah 35:1–6).

Does your situation feel like parched land? God doesn't just sprinkle it with moisture. It says that water will gush forth in the wilderness. Streams in the desert – a strange concept – reveal the goodness of our God. As we acknowledge and believe He is in control, and as we give thanks, we see things happen that seem beyond our comprehension.

Salvation means wholeness and God wants wholeness in every area of our lives. When we get free in our spirit, when we choose to respond in our spirit, we get free in our soul.

For reflection and action

- *God's comfort overflows.*
- *God works in all things for our good.*
- *Give thanks in all circumstances.*
- *Water will gush forth in the wilderness; there will be fruit in the desolate places.*

Day 22

Guilt

Guilt can be a prompting of the conscience that something is wrong in our lives, or it can be a thief in the night come to destroy our peace, resulting in insecurity and self-condemnation. There are different types of guilt: *Objective guilt* occurs when a law has been broken and we are guilty, whether we feel so or not. *Subjective guilt* is a personal feeling of discomfort, regret or remorse at having done something wrong or having failed to do something. Subjective guilt can be either true or false. *True guilt* is the feeling which occurs when we have violated a law or standard and our guilt fits our actions. *False guilt* operates from an over-sensitive conscience and does not fit our actions. False guilt can fester in our lives and cause major problems emotionally and spiritually.

True guilt – you confess, He forgives

True guilt is dealt with by recognising the nature of what we have done wrong, repenting before God, asking His forgiveness, forgiving others and forgiving ourselves. Do you wonder if what you have done wrong can ever be forgiven? "*If we confess our sins, he is faithful and just and will forgive us our sins and purify us from all unrighteousness*" (1 John 1:9). When Jesus died on the cross He paid the price for every sin in the world. The price has already been paid, but we have to claim it through confessing and receiving forgiveness. There is no question of whether God has heard your request, or whether He can forgive this particular sin. Scripture is completely clear. You confess, He forgives.

The only thing which comes between you and receiving from God is your thinking, "I don't deserve it". You're right! None of us deserves it! But that is what makes Christianity so incredible.

> "... your guilt is taken away and your sin atoned for."
> Isaiah 6:7

False guilt

Resolving false guilt involves letting go of our distorted thinking, and accepting the power of God's love and forgiveness. When God forgives He cancels the debt. Imagine you owed a huge amount of money. If you found out that someone had paid off your debt, you wouldn't then try paying it yourself would you? You would just keep thinking, "thank you, thank you, thank you". When you wonder, "How can I be forgiven", hold onto the words in Romans 10:11–12, *"Anyone who trusts in him will never be put to shame ... the same Lord is Lord of all and richly blesses all who call on him"*.

If you have not sinned but feel guilty, then you are allowing yourself to believe a lie and are moving into self-condemnation. Begin to take on board the things we have looked at over the days, believing who you are in Christ, and recognising the difference between thought patterns of God and those not of God, and allow your thinking to come in line with God's truth.

For reflection and action

- *There are different types of guilt.*
- *If you sin, confess your sin and you will be forgiven.*
- *None of us deserve to be forgiven, but we are forgiven!*
- *Allow your thinking to come in line with God's truth.*

Day 23

Confusion

"Where is God in my situation?" you may ask. "It is difficult to pray, I don't know if God can hear me". Yes He can hear and He does want to hear you. Your prayers matter to Him. He knows the situation anyway, but He loves to hear your voice. He knows your voice. Like a parent who listens for his/her child's voice, so God listens for you.

As to how to pray, I once heard someone speak about the Lord's Prayer. It begins, "Our Father" and so the foundation of prayer is that God is our Father. It then moves on to, "Hallowed be Thy name". Hallow comes from the Greek *Hagiazo*, which means to make holy, to sanctify. In other words, when you pray, sanctify God; tell Him that He is holy, that He is majestic, that you see His beauty in creation. Remember how wonderful God is.

Putting life into perspective

If we begin our prayer by praying about our problem, all we see is our problem. When we begin by praising God and lifting His name, it puts life into perspective. Out of that place of praise it is easier to come to God and ask Him for your needs to be met. Because you have spent time praising Him and looking at His character, that He is good, you will have confidence to know He will give you good things.

Surrender precedes request. If we are not surrendered to God and walking with Him as Lord of our life, we are not in a position to ask. It is easy to blame God, "You haven't answered." But there is a responsibility on our part first to surrender. Make sure that no sin comes between you and God. Sin is a separator. "*Surely the arm of the Lord is not too short to save, nor his ear too dull to hear. But your iniquities have separated you from your God ...*" (Isaiah 59:1–2).

> "... his ears are attentive to their prayer ... ."
> 1 Peter 3:12

Get to know His voice

What about how you are hearing God? God has such a tender heart and speaks words of encouragement to His children. You are His child. Are you hearing what He is saying to you at the moment? Some people feel they can't hear God. God is not withholding His voice, but are you listening? Have you learnt how to listen and to know His voice as distinct from other voices? Jesus said, *"I am the good shepherd; I know my sheep and my sheep know me"* (John 10:14). You can recognise God communicating with you. He does so in many different ways: through His Word, speaking to you, prophecy, dreams. If you are not sure of hearing God, remember that the only way you get to know someone is by spending time with that person. Get to know the character of God, pray, read the Bible, but also allow Him time to speak. His words are worth hearing and when they are personal to you, they are precious.

For reflection and action

- *God wants to hear your voice.*
- *Begin your prayer by acknowledging the holiness of God.*
- *Surrender to God.*
- *Listen to what God has to say to you.*

Day 24

Mistrust

When we get hurt it can become harder to trust people and sometimes we include God in those it is difficult to trust. "How do I know how He's going to react?" I once received a very honest letter from a young girl with whom I was corresponding. She wrote, "I tend to read your letters hearing a tone of disapproval (the same way I read the Bible), so I decided to listen to a tape of one of your seminars and then read your letter in the same tone of voice, which is caring and not condemning. It made a lot of difference. It's not quite so easy to find out what tone of voice God is using though."

God will not let us down

In reply I told her of an instance in my own life. I was about to be prayed for by a lady I had never met before. As she was approaching me God told her to treat me gently. I knew that, at a later date, the Holy Spirit would continue to minister to me on my own, but I was a little concerned about the manner in which He would do this. The person who had prayed for me said: "Don't forget, if God told me to be gentle, the Holy Spirit is not going to be anything different!"

I think that the tone of God's voice is gentler and more compassionate than any of us have ever heard in each other. It is so easy for us to allow something of us (our impatience, own agendas, etc.) to interfere when supporting someone in distress. But with God, His motive, His love, His compassion are pure. Psalm 32:10 says, *"... the Lord's unfailing love surrounds the man who trusts in him."* If we get to know the character of God we know that He will not let us down.

> "... blessed is he who trusts in the Lord."
> Proverbs 16:20

How can we trust others?

Trusting others is perhaps harder. They, unlike God, can be unpredictable. What do we do if we are hurt by others? When we get hurt we want to take the matter into our own hands; often we want to retreat or hold back from others. Self-protection is natural, but it does not help in the long run. It usually involves building a wall around ourselves. It is safe, but lonely, and not only lonely, but difficult for love to penetrate.

We need to transfer the situation into God's hands. When we do this, we let go of the burden and can allow ourselves to still move towards people despite having been hurt. When you bless the person who curses you a wall cannot be built, and so you find that there is no prison inside which you live.

For reflection and action

- *God's motive, love and compassion are pure.*
- *The Lord's unfailing love surrounds the person who trusts Him.*
- *Don't build walls of self-protection.*
- *Transfer the situation into God's hands.*

Day 25

Rejection

Rejection comes in all sorts of guises! Whatever form it takes it is not comfortable. Do you feel rejected, or different, or left out?

Rejection is so much more painful when we look to others to affirm us: when we need others as our point of reference for significance and worth. But when we know that our worth and significance, our security and identity are in God, we are more able to take rejection, because our emotional life does not depend upon what others think.

Jesus suffered too

When someone mentions the suffering of Jesus and asks us to relate it to our own suffering, sometimes it can stir up feelings of frustration, "I know He suffered, but it doesn't make me feel any better; it only makes me feel more guilty. Besides He hasn't suffered exactly what I am suffering." I used to think in this way until I realised that it was through His suffering that my suffering is dealt with.

Isaiah 53:2–5 says of Jesus, "*... He had no beauty or majesty to attract us to him, nothing in his appearance that we should desire him. He was despised and rejected by men, a man of sorrows, and familiar with suffering. Like one from whom men hide their faces he was despised, and we esteemed him not.*" If you feel like this – unattractive, despised, rejected, not esteemed – there is great hope for you. Isaiah goes on to say of Jesus, "*Surely he took up our infirmities and carried our sorrows ... he was pierced for our transgressions, he was crushed for our iniquities; the punishment that brought us peace was upon him, and by his wounds we are healed.*"

> **"I have chosen you and have not rejected you."**
> **Isaiah 41:9**

His acceptance of us

We shouldn't just say, "OK, so Jesus suffered, I haven't suffered nearly so badly and He has paid the price for me." Instead, we need to stop trying to find acceptance through others, and know deep in our heart our acceptance by God, through what Jesus has done for us. Our focus shifts from our rejection by some, to our acceptance by God. But don't just think in your head, "Fine, I'm accepted (but I don't feel it)", instead know your acceptance.

Jesus came and identified with your rejection, with your hurt, with your lack of esteem, so that you can then identify with His acceptance. Where many of us stop is after identifying with His rejection. But there is more. Let Him take your rejection and let yourself receive His acceptance. Identify with His righteousness, His holiness, His status as heir to the kingdom. In Him, and only in Him, do we have acceptance in God's eyes.

For reflection and action

- *Don't allow your emotional life to hang upon what other people think.*
- *Through Jesus' suffering your suffering has been dealt with.*
- *Jesus has identified with your rejection that you may identify with His acceptance.*
- *Live in the good of what is true for you in Him.*

Worthlessness

We often view our worth according to what the media and those around us dictate as acceptable. I am of worth when … I achieve, I am shown love, I am slim. Sometimes, even when we attain these we still don't feel of worth, and as circumstances change so our view of ourselves changes. Jesus said, "*The Spirit gives life; the flesh counts for nothing*" (John 6:63). So in other words, even if we attain a feeling of worth through our own achievements, it means nothing, it has no place, and on the day of judgment will be frizzled in the fire. Our worth is in what Christ has done for us. It's like having being given an honorary doctorate and then trying to swot for and sit the exam. You already have all you need! What counts is what you have already been given.

You are a child of God

Have you begun to catch hold of all that is yours in Christ and who you really are as you have been reading these words each day? We have already looked at some of the verses which speak the truth about you as a child of God. You can also say:

- I have the mind of Christ (1 Corinthians 2:16);
- I am being transformed into the image of Jesus (Romans 8:29);
- I am created in Jesus for good works (Ephesians 2:10);
- I have received power through the Holy Spirit (Acts 1:8).

As a result of the truth about you, you can declare:

- I can understand the things which God has freely given me (1 Corinthians 2:12);
- I can overcome Satan by the blood of Jesus and the word of my testimony (Revelation 12:11);
- I can be more than a conqueror through him who loved me (Romans 8:37);

> "We ... are being transformed into his likeness with ever-increasing glory." 2 Corinthians 3:18

- I can be filled with the knowledge of God's will in all spiritual wisdom and understanding (Colossians 1:9);
- I can walk in a manner worthy of the Lord and please Him (Colossians 1:10);
- I can bear fruit in every good work (Colossians 1:10);
- I can be strengthened with all power (Colossians 1:11).

Our true identity

Our opinion of ourselves needs to be checked against the truth of God's Word about us. In Christ we are worth much, but we have to take what we have been given by Him. You can give someone the most precious gift, but if it is never unwrapped, or unwrapped and then not used, it is worthless. It doesn't matter how little you are, it's how big God is!

What is your identity? It is as a child of God. It is to function as God designed us to function – in dependence upon Him.

For reflection and action

- The flesh counts for nothing.
- Pursue the spiritual.
- Catch hold of all that is yours in Christ.
- You are designed for dependence upon God.

Day 27

Tormented

Has temptation to fall back into a particular way of handling things been a part of the torment you face? Temptation entices us towards sin.

The sin of which we are often less aware, and yet which causes so much damage, is allowing ourselves to get between us and God. The account of King Nebuchadnezzar in Daniel 4 is a good example. Nebuchadnezzar had a dream which he asked Daniel to interpret for him. It was a warning about his pride and his need to repent. He didn't. Instead he indulged in personal glory and his pride was his downfall. Consequently, for seven years he was driven from his people and lived like a wild animal. He remained in this state of "madness" until he acknowledged *"that the Most High is sovereign over the kingdoms of men ..."* (v.32). The change came about when he took his eyes off himself and onto the Lord. *"At the end of that time, I, Nebuchadnezzar, raised my eyes towards heaven, and my sanity was restored ..."* (v. 34).

Receiving God's peace

Keeping our eyes on God, not on the problem, and holding fast to the commands of the Lord is important if you are to combat torment. Psalm 119:165 says, *"Great peace have they who love your law, and nothing can make them stumble."*

The word peace appears in almost every book in the New Testament, which shows how significant it is. The roots of peace are buried deep in Jesus Christ for He was called the Prince of Peace (Isaiah 9:6). The Hebrew word for peace, shalom, means far more than being without strife or hostility; it means well-being, security and tranquillity.

Peace was made perfect in Jesus. He was complete, and through the shedding of His blood on the cross He broke down the barrier between God and man, enabling us to be united to God in peace.

> "You will keep in perfect peace him whose mind is steadfast, because he trusts in you." Isaiah 26:3

Freedom from torment

In John 14:27 Jesus says, *"Peace I leave with you; my peace I give you. I do not give to you as the world gives. Do not let your hearts be troubled and do not be afraid."* There are several important points here: 1. The peace Jesus gives is not as the world gives; 2. Jesus does not say "the peace I give to some", He says, "my peace I give you"; 3. Following His words about the peace He gives are words about not letting your heart be troubled and not being afraid. The result of receiving God's peace in our lives is a freedom from troubled and fearful hearts.

One of the things we can think is, "God might not want to give me peace". Psalm 29:11 says, *"... the Lord blesses his people with peace."* It is significant that the psalmist chooses the word bless to be associated with peace. Blessing signifies an imparting; something is given over which cannot be taken back. When God blesses us with His peace – He blesses us with His peace whether we believe it or not!

For reflection and action

- *Resist temptation.*
- *Change comes about when you take your eyes off yourself and put them on the Lord.*
- *Keep the commands of the Lord.*
- *Loose the peace of God into your life.*

Nightmare

Day 28

"My child, I was there in the middle of the nightmare – that period in your life when everything seemed to go wrong. Wherever you turned there were problems. Despair gripped you, didn't it? You felt as if you were entirely lost.

"I was there when you even contemplated suicide. It was I who stayed your hand, for I would not want you to destroy yourself, so great is my love for you.

"This was the most difficult time of your life, wasn't it? But you came through, my child, because I was there with you in the middle of it all. When you pass through the waters, I have promised they will not overwhelm you. When you go through the fire, you will not be burned.

"I never left you"

"I know how deeply hurt you felt at the time. You were experiencing a desolation such as Jesus experienced for you on the cross when He cried out, 'My God, my God, why have you forsaken me?' You felt forsaken, didn't you? Yet I was there all the time. I never left you.

"I know the hurts that were inflicted upon you by others. I know also that those to whom you turned could not understand your dilemma. You see, they had never been where you had been. It seemed you were at the bottom of a great pit and nobody knew how to lift you out. But I came, didn't I? I heard your cry. I came and rescued you and lifted you up. I held you in my loving arms. I saw the joy slowly beginning to come back into your heart. I saw the peace gradually filling your soul; and I rejoiced.

"Forgive"

"It took some time, didn't it? But did you notice the point at which everything began to change? It was when you forgave. I watched you sink down a spiritual well, and resentment ate at your heart. You felt you had

I Was There in the Nightmare

been dealt with so unjustly; one injustice seemed to be heaped on another. People turned against you and insulted you.

"You cried out to me for vengeance. That is not what I tell you to do. Forgive, love your enemies and pray for those who persecute you. I had to wait until you were obedient to my word. I kept you through those difficult months until you began to rejoice in me and give thanks, even in those dire circumstances. Then everything began to change, didn't it? Have you learned the lesson well, my child?

"In future, when others oppose and hurt you, will you let a root of bitterness spring up? Or will you be merciful and forgive? Instead of crying out to me in a rage of self-righteousness, will you praise me, knowing that I am the God of justice and that I vindicate my chosen ones?

"I honour the truth and those who hold fast to my Word. In my love, I cannot save you from the battles that lie ahead of you; but I shall always be at your side and my Spirit will work within you for your good."[4]

For reflection and action

- God is with you in the nightmare.
- You are going to come through because God is with you.
- God holds you in His loving arms.
- God's Spirit will work within you for good.

Day 29

Unforgiveness

On Day 16, when we looked at Endlessness, I spoke of how God had worked in my life at a particular time of distress and how shortly prior to this time God had shown me something I needed to put in order. What was it? Unforgiveness.

The need to forgive

God had already told me I needed to forgive. I knew that not doing so was holding me back and so I forgave. The importance of this became clear after I prayed with the lady he had sent. God had given this person two pages of a book for me to read. Lending me the book, and not telling me that God had spoken to her, I began reading. I stopped and started praying that God would show me which section to read. He led me to the same two pages. The words are from Colin Urquhart's book *My Dear Child*, the words you read yesterday: "I Was There in the Nightmare".

Yes, God was with me in my nightmare. He never left me and was the only one who fully understood the situation. But the change in me began when I chose to forgive. That seems hard doesn't it? People treat you unjustly and everything inside you screams for vengeance. If not vengeance then at least that others should know what you have faced. I went down the path of unforgiveness and at the end of it I found no stream in the desert. Instead I found the twisted roots of bitterness which had a stranglehold on me.

Why is forgiveness so important? Because if you do not forgive you are the one who remains in bondage. You remain bound to the one not forgiven.

Choose to forgive

Jesus was betrayed, rejected, flogged so that He was barely recognisable, and hurt by even those close to Him, and yet He forgave. His disciple, Peter,

> **"Forgive as the Lord forgave you."**
> **Colossians 3:13**

denied three times that he even knew Jesus and Jesus looked at him with love – that was supernatural love. "But He was the Son of God, it's different for Him", we can say. What we tend to forget is that His suffering was endured in His humanity. He was fully human, yet fully God. It is not normal to forgive following such treatment. The reason He could forgive was that He had the power of God flowing through Him. We have the same power. The power that raised Christ from the dead, is within you. That is power!

If we try to forgive in our own strength we can't do it. We can only do it through the power of God. Our part is making the choice. You don't feel like doing it, but you choose to do so and you know that something will happen in the spiritual realm.

For reflection and action

- The path of unforgiveness leads to bitterness.
- If you do not forgive you remain in bondage.
- Don't try to forgive in your own strength.
- Something happens when you choose to forgive.

Day 30

Next?

We've been together for a month now. Quite a journey wasn't it? Perhaps you are only just beginning to move on, or perhaps you have moved on a long way. It doesn't matter. The important thing is that you are moving. If you are progressing, then your progress delights God. Zephaniah 3:17 reminds us, *"The Lord your God is with you, he is mighty to save. He will take great delight in you, he will quiet you with his love, he will rejoice over you with singing."* God is rejoicing over you!

Put it into action!

What if nothing seems to have changed? You may have to seek God for an answer. I will tell you what happened in my situation though. There was a time when nothing changed for the better, in fact it became much worse. I had prayed with someone and she had spoken the Word of God into my life. I went back at a later date feeling terrible, hoping for a fresh revelation and a tender touch. Instead she said, "Did you do what I said?" "No," I replied. "If you don't take the medicine, you don't get better," were her parting words. I went home and ran to God. From that day on it began to change. If necessary go back over this book, but certainly read the Bible, pray, and put into action all that we have looked at together.

Sometimes what holds us back from moving forward is our need to understand. We cannot always understand the ways or workings of God. Hebrews 11:1 tells us, *"Now faith is being sure of what we hope for and certain of what we do not see."* If we wait until we know, feel, have proof, we will not see faith in evidence and we will not see the fruit of faith. The only way you learn about faith is to step out in faith. There are three stages: You hear the Word; you believe what you hear; you act on what you hear.

> "There is surely a future hope for you, and your hope will not be cut off." Proverbs 23:18

Never give up

You may not believe, having confessed your sin, that you are forgiven. But the Word says that you are forgiven, therefore you believe you are forgiven and act in the truth that you are forgiven. If you are forgiven, you do not live in shame and sorrow and self-punishment. The same principle applies in all other areas of your life. Never give up on something that God hasn't given up on.

For reflection and action

- *God rejoices over your progress.*
- *Take in the truth.*
- *Step out in faith.*
- *Never give up!*

References

1. *The Bondage Breaker*, Neil T. Anderson, Monarch, 1993.
2. Ibid.
3. *The Truth That Sets You Free*, Colin Urquhart, Hodder & Stoughton, 1993, p. 143.
4. *My Dear Child*, Colin Urquhart, Hodder & Stoughton, 1990, pp. 144–145.

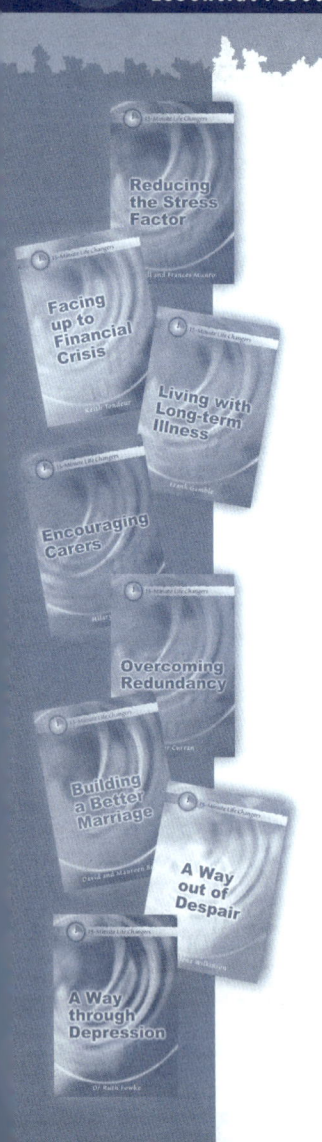

15 Minute Life Changers –
Essential resources for leaders and carers.

Each title £1.25 each

Previously published as the New Perspectives series.

Reducing the Stress Factor
Learn how to deal with stress biblically and effectively.
ISBN: 1-85345-217-3

Facing up to Financial Crisis
Learn how to deal with finances from a biblical perspective.
ISBN: 1-85345-214-9

Living with a Long-term Illness
Discover how to also live in the truth that "...in all things God works for the good of those who love Him."
ISBN: 1-85345-222-X

Overcoming Redundancy
Face this difficult time by taking the initiative and celebrating your God-given gifts. ISBN: 1-85345-216-5

A Way out of Despair
Address issues of despair, including suicide, rejection, guilt, self-hate. ISBN: 1-85345-218-1

Encouraging Carers
This book helps carers to understand that their strength can be found in God. ISBN: 1-85345-219-X

Building a Better Marriage
A helpful aid for people experiencing a difficult patch, or more serious issues in their marriage. ISBN: 1-85345-213-0

A Way through Depression
Biblical wisdom to help anyone suffering from this debilitating condition. ISBN: 1-85345-221-1

Prices correct at time of printing